Autism and Me

by Amy Howard

Autism and Me
Text copyright © Amy Howard 2019
Illustrations by Marta Kwasniewska
Illustrations copyright © Gatehouse Media Limited 2019
Edited by Catherine White

First published and distributed in 2019 by Gatehouse Media Limited

ISBN: 978-1-84231-184-4

British Library Cataloguing-in-Publication Data:
A catalogue record for this book is available from the British Library

No part of this publication may be reproduced in any form or by any means, electronic, mechanical, photocopying, recording or otherwise, without the prior written consent of the publishers.

Introduction

My name is Amy. I live in Coventry and I am 38 years old. This is the first story I have written. I enjoyed writing it. It was very emotional for me.

My confidence has improved in the last two years. I never could have written a story two years ago.

The story is called *Autism and Me*. My friend Bengy and I discussed the contents of the story. I then typed it up at the learning hub. Once I had typed up the story, Natasha, my teacher at Crisis, helped me with the grammar and punctuation.

Amy

Some people don't understand autism,
they don't show me respect,
and they are not very nice about me.

Autism sometimes makes me angry,
especially when I find housing benefit forms,
and other forms, hard.

When I became homeless,
the people at the council confused me
and it upset me.

I was sofa surfing.
They didn't explain things to me properly,
so it took me a long time to get help.

HOUSING BENEFIT OFFICE
HOUSING BENEFIT APPLICATION FORM

Not everyone understands autism,
so can confuse me and make me upset
without meaning to.
I am writing this story
so people can understand me
and my autism better.

Because of my autism
I have claustrophobia.
I don't like too many people
and I get very scared in large crowds.

Since I joined Crisis,
I have grown in confidence.
I talk to myself every day and say:
"Everything is going to be okay, Amy."

If I do panic in a crowd,
I now try to deal with it.
I take deep breaths, rub my chest
and remember it's only anxiety.

Sometimes I get angry and upset.
I used to get really angry
when people didn't understand.
I would shout at people,
which didn't help.

They didn't know it was because of my autism.
They just thought I was angry.
I would always feel guilty afterwards
and say sorry.

Now I don't keep things bottled up.
I ask people to listen carefully
and I try to use positive body language.

If I get really angry I go outside,
take deep breaths and calm down.
If I need to, I'll talk to my friends
or support worker.

At my home, when I'm okay,
I put my thumb up.
When I'm not okay,
I will talk to the staff about it.

They remind me that everybody
has good days and bad days.

When I don't know directions
I feel disorientated.
I struggle to find places by directions alone
and prefer people to show me in person.

I try to be on time,
but my time keeping can be poor.
My challenge is to get up an hour earlier
so I can try to be on time
for my appointments and classes.

It's good to work with people
who understand my autism,
because they support me and don't judge.

BZZZT

Fluorescent lighting affects my eyes,
so I have to wear my sunglasses indoors
sometimes.

If I am in a large crowd
and people talk over each other,
and I don't get a word in,
I put my earmuffs on
and it drowns out the noise.

This helps me to stay calm in situations
and not struggle with the sensory overload.

Although I am autistic,
it does not define me.
I am much more.

My family and friends always say positive
and nice things about me,
and I have achieved a lot
over the past year.

I love the actor Dan Stevens
and I'm an official Dan Stevens fan.
I like walking and playing badminton.
I travelled to London for the very first time
this year.

I am good at reading
and my teacher says I am a great speller!
I enjoy writing, but this is my first story.

I love word searches and, eventually,
I would like to help people
with their reading and spelling too,
maybe even start a spelling group.

I am not a failure, I am a success
and I won't let people say otherwise.
I am a very positive person
and I hope people will read this
and feel happy for me.

I hope it will help them
to understand autism a bit better.

There's no such word as can't in this world.
You can do things, even if they are hard.

Crisis, my best friend Bengy,
Chosen Lives and the residents at my home
are all very supportive.

I am a work in progress
just like everyone else.
But sometimes,
I just need a little extra support.

Afterword

Crisis Coventry is a charity that works with people who are homeless or who have experienced homelessness. The members who attend my Creative Writing class have all either been housed recently or are still living in interim accommodation, such as hostels, hotels or National Asylum Support Service (NASS) accommodation.

When Amy came to us, she was experiencing serious social isolation with no support from statutory services. Through working with the team at Crisis, she is now securely housed and is attending lots of wonderful group activities with different organisations across the city.

Amy had never written anything before, so the idea of creative writing was a new concept to her. We discussed what she would want to write about and she decided she wanted to create a story that would help people to understand her better, and perhaps help them to understand other people with autism too.

This piece was written over a period of three weeks and, when Amy started writing, it just poured out of her. As you can probably tell, I'm a very proud teacher. I hope you enjoy it as much as we have here at Crisis.

Natasha Reilly

Creative Writing Teacher, Crisis Coventry

Gatehouse Books®

Our writers are adults who are developing their basic reading and writing skills. Their ideas and experiences make fascinating material for any reader, but are particularly relevant for adults working on their own reading and writing skills. The writing often strikes a chord with the reader - a shared experience of struggling against many odds.

The format of our books is clear and uncluttered.
The language is familiar and the text is often line-broken, so that each line ends at a natural pause.

Gatehouse Books are widely used within Adult Basic Education throughout the English speaking world. They are also a valuable resource within the Prison Education Service and Probation Services, Social Services and secondary schools - in both basic skills and ESOL teaching.

Contact us

Gatehouse Media Limited
PO Box 965
Warrington
WA4 9DE

Tel: 01925 267778
E-mail: info@gatehousebooks.com
Website: www.gatehousebooks.com